FRIGHTFUL
FIRST
WORLD
WAR

TERRY DEARY

ILLUSTRATED BY **MARTIN BROWN**

To Private John Condon, Royal Irish Regiment.
Died 24 May 1915, aged 14 years old.
The youngest British soldier to die during the First World War.

Scholastic Children's Books,
Euston House, 24 Eversholt Street,
London NW1 1DB, UK

A division of Scholastic Ltd
London ~ New York ~ Toronto ~ Sydney ~ Auckland
Mexico City ~ New Delhi ~ Hong Kong

First published in the UK by Scholastic Ltd, 1998
This abridged edition published 2013
This edition published 2018

Text © Terry Deary, 1998, 2013
Illustrations © Martin Brown, 1998, 2013
Cover line and colour by Robin Henley, 2018
Index by Caroline Hamilton

Scholastic Ltd gratefully acknowledges permission to reprint the extract from *All Quiet on the Western Front* by
Erich Maria Remarque, published by The Bodley Head.

ISBN 978 1407 17845 5

Printed and bound in the UK by CPI Group (UK) Ltd, Croydon, CR0 4YY

The right of Terr_ Deary and Martin Brown to be identified as the author and illustrator o_ his work
respectively has b___ _____ by them in accordance with the Copyright, Designs and Paten__ Act, 1988.

This book is sold sub___ ___ __ the condition that it shall not, by way of trade or otherwise be le__ resold, hired
out, or otherwise ci_____ _____ consent in any form or binding oth__ than that in
which it is publisl____ _____ upon the

Papers used ___ J940.3 JUNIOR NON-FI _____ grown in sustainable _____ ests.

www.scholastic.co.uk

Contents

Introduction

History can be horrible. So horrible that some boring old fogies think young people should not be told the whole, terrible truth.

But if you never learn the truth, you'll miss out on some of the most useful things in life...

> MY GRANDAD SAYS SOLDIERS SOFTENED THEIR BOOTS WITH SWEET PEA MIXTURE. WHAT'S THAT?

> SWEET PEAS ARE FLOWERS. NOW GET ON WITH YOUR WORK

And the next time your new leather shoes hurt you, stuff them full of flowers. What happens? Nothing. The shoes stay hard and your feet get blisters.

Why couldn't your teachers tell you the truth about 'sweet pea' mixture? Either…

a) they don't know or

b) they know … but they are too embarrassed to say.

What you need is a book that's not too embarrassed to tell you about the awful things people used to do. You want a history of the horrible.

And it's no use telling you…

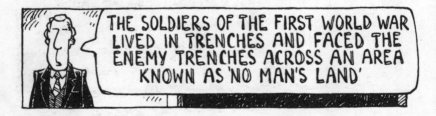

THE SOLDIERS OF THE FIRST WORLD WAR LIVED IN TRENCHES AND FACED THE ENEMY TRENCHES ACROSS AN AREA KNOWN AS 'NO MAN'S LAND'

That makes it sound cosy and peaceful, doesn't it? The truth is pretty nasty, but you'll never understand how those people suffered unless you read

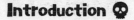

their own true memories of trenches and no man's land…

> Bodies and bits of bodies, and clots of blood, and green metallic-looking slime made by the explosive gases were floating on the surface of the water. Our men lived there and died there within a few yards of the enemy. They crouched below the sandbags and burrowed into the sides of trenches. Lice crawled over them in swarms. If they dug to get deeper cover, their shovels went into the softness of dead bodies who had been their friends. Scraps of flesh, booted legs, blackened hands, eyeless heads came falling over them when the enemy fired shells at their position.

That's more like the truth because it was written by a soldier who was there.

Of all the history in the world the story of the First World War – also known as the Great War – is perhaps the most horrible. It's a story of what happens when machines go to war and human beings get in the way. But it's also a story of courage and craziness, brave people and batty people, friendships and fierce hatreds, love … and lice.

8

The Great War gangs

Why did the Great War start? Lots of big, thick history books have been written to answer that question. But, to put it simply, by 1914 the countries of Europe had formed themselves into two big gangs … like street gangs. The gang called the 'Central Powers' was led by the Germans and the gang we call the 'Allies' was led by the French and British.

The two gangs started collecting weapons, making threats and swapping insults, the way gangs do.

All it needed was for one gang member to throw the first stone and a huge punch-up would follow.

The Black Hand bunglers

So exactly *how* did the First World War start? It's never one of the gang leaders that starts the fight, is it? It's always one of the scruffy little kids that hangs around the edge. In this case, the scruffy little kid was called Bosnia in the Allies' gang.

And so a Serbian gang known as the Black Hand (honest!) waited 'til the Emperor came to Bosnia. Gavrilo Princip was a Serbian Black Hand freedom fighter.

The first stone had been thrown. Austria declared war on Serbia, and Germany helped Austria so Russia helped Serbia so France helped Russia. Germany marched through Belgium to get to France so Britain helped Belgium.

The First World War had started. It was expected to last about four months but it lasted four frightful years.

But, before the war starts, here are two quick questions:

1 What happened to Ferdi's blood-soaked jacket after his death?

a) It was taken into battle like a flag for the Austrians to follow.

b) He was buried in it.

c) It was put in a museum, so gruesome people could go and gaze at it.

2 What happened to the assassin Gavrilo Princip?

a) He was shot by the police as he ran away.

b) He escaped and lived happily ever after.

c) He was arrested and put in prison.

Answers

1c) Franz Ferdinand's death was the start of the bloodiest war seen until that time. So his blood-soaked coat was an important reminder of the terrible event. It is now on display at the Austrian Military Museum in Vienna, Austria. Go and see it ... if you like that sort of thing.

2c) Gavrilo Princip was taken alive. His two shots killed millions and millions of people. Yet he was allowed to live. Just as the First World War reached an end, gunman Gavrilo died in prison of a lung disease. Pity it didn't get him four years before!

Wacky Willie

Things may have stayed calm and the Serbian trouble could have died down. But some of the leaders of the gangs weren't too bright and weren't too pleasant. Take the German monarch…

Title: Kaiser Wilhelm

Job: Monarch of Germany

Peculiarity:
Unpopular. Nobody liked poor Willy. His grandmother, Queen Victoria of Britain, couldn't stand him. His (English) mother refused to wish him a happy birthday … so he sulked for days. His father thought he would be a dangerous leader — smart dad!

Weakness: He was born with a withered left arm and it embarrassed him. When he was photographed, he insisted on hiding his weak arm. People around him hid their strong left arms, too.

Nasty streak: German workers went on strike and he ordered soldiers to attack the strikers. 'I expect my troops to shoot at least 500,' he said.

Most likely to say: I hate everybody.

Least likely to say: Let's talk calmly about this.

1914 – The Year of the First Shot

No one is surprised when a war breaks out in August 1914. Germany smashed France in the Franco–Prussian War of 1871 and it was just a matter of time before France tried to take its revenge. But people are surprised that the war is still going on by the end of 1914. The two sides are like two heavyweight boxers jumping into the ring. Each one expects a quick knockout. But they will end up slugging it out, toe to toe, 'til they are exhausted.

Timeline 1914
28 June

Archduke Franz Ferdinand is assassinated in Bosnia. Austria is very annoyed because he was going to be their next emperor. (Franz is too dead to be annoyed.)

23 July

Austria blames Serbia for the death of Ferdi because the assassins were from Serbia. Serbia grovels but its apology is not accepted. This means WAR.

4 August

The German army marches through Belgium to attack France, so Britain joins the war to help 'poor little Belgium'.

23 August

Meanwhile, in the east, the German army defeats the Russian army. Round one to Germany.

9 September

The French stop the Germans at the Battle of the Marne. Round two to France.

October

Millions rush to join the armies. They're afraid it will be over before Christmas and before they can fight. It *will* be over before Christmas … 1918.

22 November

The Allies and the Central Powers have battered one another to a standstill in northern France. They dig 'trenches' opposite one another ... and won't move from them much for four years. No winners – only soldiers lose ... their lives.

25 December

Enemies stop fighting for a day or two, and even play friendly football matches. It can't last, and it won't be repeated.

"DID YOU KNOW...?
THE FIRST BRITS TO FIGHT IN THE FIRST WORLD WAR FOUGHT IN LONDON! ON 2 AUGUST 1914, TWO DAYS BEFORE WAR WAS DECLARED, PEACE MARCHERS CLASHED WITH LONDONERS WHO WANTED WAR.**"**

True lies

When you go to war, you can't fight against nice people, can you? You have to believe the enemy are real slime-balls who would murder your granny and poison your gerbil if they won. You have to learn to *hate* them.

In Germany, a new national anthem was written called the 'Hymn of Hate'. And when people met a friend in the street, they no longer said, '*Güten Morgen*' (good morning) they said, '*Gott strafe England*' (God punish England). These words were rubber-stamped on letters, printed on millions of postcards and engraved on badges and brooches.

Meanwhile, in the UK, the music of German composers was banned. (Since many had died some years before the war, they won't have been too upset.)

And if your enemy wasn't nasty enough, what could you do? You could invent a few lies about them. So, it was widely believed that German grocers in Britain had poisoned food and that German barbers were cutting their customers' throats and secretly dumping the bodies. Here's what the enemies said about one other … but can you spot the lies?

1 Brits believed the German soldiers were monsters…

IN BELGIUM BRITISH NURSES ARE BEING CARVED WITH KNIVES AND LEFT TO DIE IN BURNING HOSPITALS. AND GERMAN SOLDIERS HAVE BEEN THROWING UP BABIES, CATCHING THEM ON BAYONETS, ROASTING THEM AND EATING THEM

SO WHAT DO THEY TASTE LIKE SIR?

2 And the Germans believed the British were just as bad…

3 Germans believed foreign visitors were spies…

4 And the Brits didn't even trust their allies!

5 The Brits certainly didn't trust their own businessmen…

6 While the Germans knew who was to blame for starting the war...

7 The Germans also believed the most amazing tales of heroic deeds...

8 Brits were sure the Germans were desperate for materials – especially fat…

9 They were also sure that Germany was running short of fighting men…

Every one of these stories was believed – and every one was false, of course. Some were deliberate lies but others were simple mistakes. Take the story of corpses being melted to make oil. It appeared in a German newspaper report from the Western Front in April 1917...

We are passing the great Kadaver Exploitation Department of this Army Group. The fat that is won here is turned into lubricating oils and everything else is ground down in the bone mills into a powder which is used for mixing with pig food – nothing can be permitted to go to waste.

Brits called corpses 'cadavers' and thought the Germans were melting *human* corpses. In German, 'Kadaver' means an *animal* corpse. The corpses being melted down were horses.

The 'Fat King'

The Brits needed fat extractors too. Major Ellis – known to soldiers as the 'Fat King' – invented a 'fat extracting' plant and set it up on the French coast. This factory took waste food, dead horses and animal waste and turned it into fat. This was sent across the Channel to be made into glycerine – an important part of TNT explosives. Nine thousand tonnes of fat were produced by the 'Fat King's' factory.

So, a horse could be killed by a German shell (no, the army 'shells' were not like winkle shells you find on the beach. They were huge exploding bombs fired from large guns), turned into TNT and fired back at them! A perfect revenge!

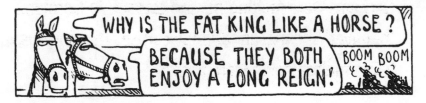

WHY IS THE FAT KING LIKE A HORSE?
BECAUSE THEY BOTH ENJOY A LONG REIGN!
BOOM BOOM

Christmas crack-shots

The First World War was the first war to see aircraft used. To begin with they would fly over enemy armies and photograph their positions or bomb them. Then the defenders sent fighters to shoot down these spy planes. War in the air had begun.

Aeroplanes also meant Brits in their homes were no longer safe in a foreign war. Londoners discovered this after just four months...

FOE FLIERS FLEE

Londoners had hopes of a quiet Christmas crushed when two German planes flew up the Thames yesterday. Crowds gathered in the streets to watch as two gallant airmen from our Royal Flying Corps chased the intruders at speeds of up to 70 miles an hour!

'I could hear the gunfire quite clearly,' a resident of Chiswick told our reporter. 'What if one of those bullets landed on an innocent head?' The aircraft observers had fired rifles at one another – a common sight in the skies over France these days. No one was hurt and the horrid Huns hurried back to Germany with their tails between their legs. But the use of guns is a deadly development of war in the air. In the early days of the war observers would carry a supply of bricks and try to drop one on to the enemy.

Londoners have been ordered to dim their lights this evening in case the unwanted visitors return. It has been reported that the Germans have invented steel darts to be dropped from their aircraft. If these strike a man they will split him in half from head to foot. Is there no end to the atrocious cruelty of this enemy?

'It just makes the people of Britain all the more determined to win,' a shop assistant from Wapping told our reporter. 'I am sending my Bobby down to the recruiting office today.'

❝DID YOU KNOW...?
IN THE SECOND WORLD WAR (1939–45)
THERE WERE SIRENS TO WARN PEOPLE OF
AIR RAIDS. BUT WHEN
AIR RAIDS BECAME
COMMON IN THE FIRST
WORLD WAR, MANY
DEFENCE CHIEFS IN
BRITAIN SENT OUT A
LETTER SAYING...❞

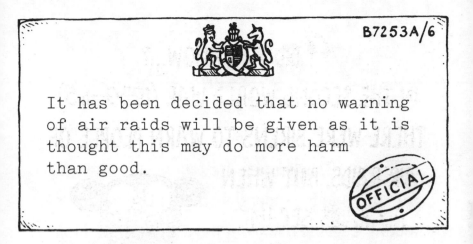

B7253A/6

It has been decided that no warning of air raids will be given as it is thought this may do more harm than good.

OFFICIAL

So, you could be walking to school and the first thing you know about the air raid is when you wake up dead.

Is this a record?

On 21 December 1914, William Gilligan, aged 41, joined the West Yorkshire Regiment at Hull. The next day, he deserted at York!

1915 – The Year of Total War

From 1915, battles are fought from trenches dug into the ground – where these battles are fought becomes known as the Western Front. Meanwhile the war spreads around the world. It is also the year of new weapons to kill new targets ... including people in their homes!

People at home can't fight back but they can take it out on foreigners living in their country (known as 'aliens', but not to be confused with little green beings from Mars!). So, in the East End of London, German shops are looted and, in one riot, German pianos are thrown from houses on to the road. A street concert is held where patriotic songs are sung. The government is forced to imprison enemy aliens for their own protection as well as to stop them spying.

In Germany anyone with 'a well-cut coat, a well-filled wallet and a notably good car' is arrested as a spy. All British people are rounded up and most are imprisoned.

Timeline 1915
19 January

First Zeppelin airship raids on Britain. Women and children, cats and dogs are in this war, like it or not.

2 February

Germany says it will surround Britain with submarines, sink food-supply ships and starve Britain to defeat.

18 March

British Government asks women to sign up for war work. Many do and they start doing it better than the men did!

22 April

Nasty new weapon, poisoned gas, first used against soldiers in the trenches.

May

Allies try to sneak round the back of the German front by landing in Gallipoli, Turkey. They expect the Turks will be a pushover.

7 May

German submarines sink a passenger ship, the *Lusitania* – on board are 128 Americans who are not even part of the war yet. Big mistake, Germany.

7 June

Zeppelin airship shot down over Flanders, northern France. That slow-moving bag of gas makes Zeppelins easy targets.

July

The Turkish state uses war as an excuse to wipe out an entire race of people, the Armenians. A step

on the road to the terrors of the Second World War.

August

Food getting short, especially in Germany. Prices go up and taxes go up to pay for the war – £1 million a day in Britain is needed to pay for the fighting.

September

At the Battle of Loos in Flanders, some brave Brits dribble a football towards enemy lines. The ball was found riddled with bullets. Like the foolhardy footballers.

12 October

Nurse Edith Cavell is caught helping Brit prisoners to escape in Belgium. She says, 'If I had to, I'd do it all over again.' Germans shoot her so she can't.

11 November

Brit minister Winston Churchill gets sacked because his Gallipoli idea is a disaster. He'll be back.

20 December

Allies give up on the Gallipoli attack and retreat. It was a very bloody mistake.

Pests and plagues

Soldiers had more to fear than enemy weapons. Creepy-crawlies and deadly diseases could kill you just as dead.

Fierce flies

At Gallipoli, flies in the summer of 1915 were very bad because of the number of unburied bodies. One soldier of the Australia and New Zealand Army Corps (Anzacs) wrote home about the flies…

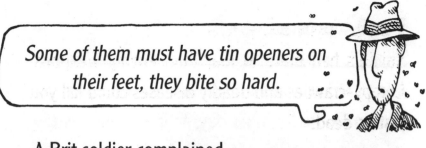

Some of them must have tin openers on their feet, they bite so hard.

A Brit soldier complained…

In order to eat your food you had to wave your hand over it then bite suddenly, otherwise a fly came with it. Any bit of food uncovered was blotted out of sight by flies in a couple of seconds.

That fly had probably had a picnic on a dead donkey a few minutes before, so it's no wonder the troops suffered so much disease in Gallipoli.

Deadly doctors

Since Florence Nightingale's work in the Crimean War of 1856, it was a little safer in war hospitals. Back in Florrie Nightie's day, a wound could easily get infected – if the bullet didn't kill you then the germs did. But doctors could still be pretty clumsy. One soldier reported...

An Anzac soldier, Private O'Connor, was wounded in the leg and captured. He was taken to Istanbul where an Armenian doctor operated to amputate O'Connor's leg. The doctor sawed halfway through the bone, grew too tired, and snapped off the rest.

SNAP

Frightful first aid

In the middle of a battle you couldn't pop down to the local chemist shop for an aspirin or dial 999 for an ambulance. Soldiers had to look after each other and they all carried a small first-aid pack into battle. Brit soldiers also had a book, *The Field Almanac 1915*, that gave some advice.

There are some instructions you may *not* like to follow next time you are flattened in a fierce football match...

Nº 27   *British Army Field Almanac 1915*

Broken limbs:
Gently put the broken limb straight after cutting off the clothes. Then fix it in this position by means of a splint made from a rifle, a roll of newspapers, bayonets, swords, pieces of wood.

A roll of newspapers! In a battle? What newspaper could be as tough as a wooden splint? The *Daily Telegraph-pole* perhaps?

By 1918, because of severe shortages in Germany, soldiers were forced to use bandages made from crêpe paper and tied on with thread.

F-f-f-f-frostbite

Frostbite is another problem you may suffer in school sports (especially during cricket matches in Britain). Again, you wouldn't want to suffer the 1915 cure...

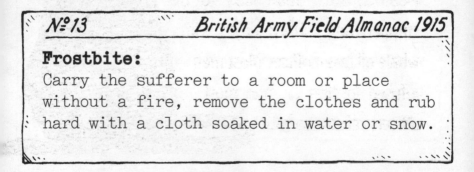

№ 13   *British Army Field Almanac 1915*

Frostbite:
Carry the sufferer to a room or place without a fire, remove the clothes and rub hard with a cloth soaked in water or snow.

Brrrr!

And the way of preventing frostbite was even worse...

In the winter of 1914–15, anti-frostbite grease was supplied in 2-lb tins to soldiers on the Western Front. It looked like lard and it contained mostly pork fat. After 1915, whale oil was issued in rum jars. This was little used because of the terrible smell. Army orders said that, before going out on patrol in cold or wet weather, each man was to be stripped and rubbed down with whale oil by an officer. Most men refused to strip ... and most officers refused to rub!

Putrid poisons

The army listed three types of poisoning. The emergency cure for 'corrosive' poisoning looks weird...

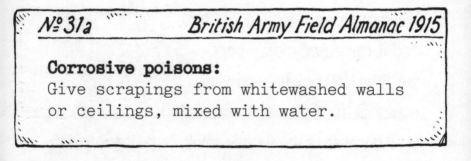

№ 31a   *British Army Field Almanac 1915*

Corrosive poisons:
Give scrapings from whitewashed walls or ceilings, mixed with water.

Perhaps the advice to eat walls is not so surprising. After all, Wall's makes ice cream and sausages!

Gruesome gas

A new First World War danger was gas attack. Orders went out from army headquarters...

If you are caught in a gas attack:

1 Take out your handkerchief.

2 Urinate into the material 'til it is soaked.

3 Tie it round your mouth and nose and breathe through it.

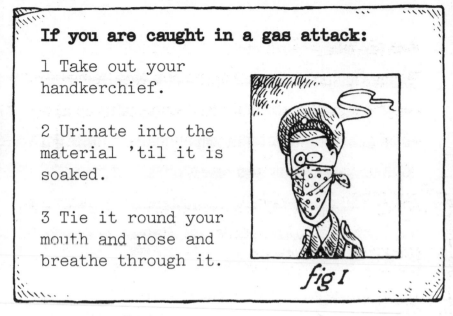

fig I

The orders didn't say what you should do if you didn't feel like a pee!

Crafty cordite

Soldiers wishing to appear unwell and thus avoid duty would chew cordite, an explosive taken from their rifle bullets. Cordite gave the soldier a high temperature but the effect soon wore off.

Lovely lice

At the Gallipoli battles, the soldiers were forced to wear the same clothes for weeks without ever taking them off. One Australian soldier finally got to take his socks off and saw a ghastly sight...

And, Ma, I swear that as I dropped my socks on the floor I saw them start to move! They were a seething mass of lice!

In the trenches, the soldiers found 'chatting' was a peaceful way to pass the quiet times. But 'chatting' didn't mean talking. It meant getting rid of the 'chats' or lice from the seams of their tunics.

One soldier compared lice to an army that had invaded his body...

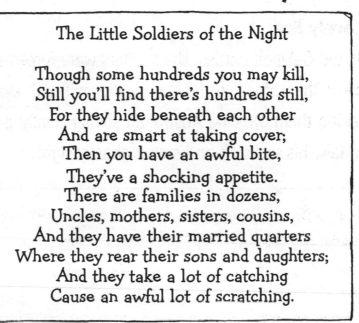

The Little Soldiers of the Night

Though some hundreds you may kill,
Still you'll find there's hundreds still,
For they hide beneath each other
And are smart at taking cover;
Then you have an awful bite,
They've a shocking appetite.
There are families in dozens,
Uncles, mothers, sisters, cousins,
And they have their married quarters
Where they rear their sons and daughters;
And they take a lot of catching
Cause an awful lot of scratching.

German soldiers described another way of dealing with their bloodsucking friends. They took the lid from a boot-polish tin and held it by a piece of wire over a candle. When the lid began to glow they'd simply drop the lice on the red-hot tin. The sizzle of the frying lice was a sweet sound to their ears.

❝ DID YOU KNOW...? BRITISH SOLDIERS SUFFERED FROM LICE THAT WERE A PALE FAWN COLOUR, BUT GERMAN SOLDIERS HAD RED LICE. IF THEY'D BRED THE TWO TOGETHER THEY COULD HAVE HAD PRETTY PINK LICE! ❞

Seriously spooky

When your life is in danger, you start to believe in 'luck'. People in danger can be very superstitious. A few new beliefs sprang up in the First World War.

Super superstitions
Bullet-proof Bibles

Pocket-sized copies of the New Testament suddenly sold tens of thousands of copies. They were being bought by anxious Brit mothers for their sons. There were stories of bullets being stopped by these little Bibles. There may have been one or two true cases of Bibles stopping 'spent' rifle bullets. They were not a lot of good against high explosive shells and machine-gun bullets.

God's people

Each side believed that they were in the right; that meant that God would be on their side. The Germans even went to war with a belt buckle that read, '*Gott mit uns*' (God with us). British soldiers saw the word 'uns' and thought that proved what they knew – they were fighting the Huns! One very popular belief was that either God had your name and number on a bullet ... or he didn't. So, you may as well charge that machine-gun. After the war, one soldier said...

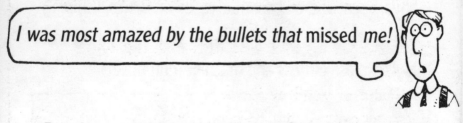

I was most amazed by the bullets that missed *me!*

But the most dangerous superstition of all was that 'Prayer can turn bullets aside'.

For the soldiers who didn't believe in God or luck, there was always this common-sense advice. It was a notice passed around the trenches...

Don't worry
When you are a soldier you can be in one of two places:
A dangerous place or a safe place.
If you're in a safe place ... don't worry.
If you're in a dangerous place you can be one of two things:
One is wounded and the other is not.
If you're not wounded ... don't worry.
If you are wounded it can be dangerous or slight:
If it's slight ... don't worry.
If it's dangerous then one of two things will happen:
You'll die or you'll recover.
If you recover ... don't worry.
If you die ... you can't worry.
In these circumstances a soldier never worries.

The Third Man

The reason for this belief was that it was a dangerous thing to do in the trenches where an enemy sniper might be watching. First light will catch his eye, second light he'll fix his sights on the light and third light … he'll pull the trigger.

The blasted statue

In the town of Albert, Flanders, there was a fine
church with a golden statue of the Virgin Mary on top.
Early in 1915, the tower was damaged and the statue
toppled over but didn't fall. For months it hung there
as the war dragged on and the British defenders in
Albert invented a strange superstition…

WHEN THE STATUE FALLS THE WAR WILL END!

If the statue fell, the British soldiers would be terribly
discouraged, so the army set up strong cables to hold
the Virgin Mary in her perilous place. For over three
years the Germans failed to knock her off her perch
and for three more years the war went on.

In 1918, the Germans finally captured the town and started using the top of the church tower as an observation post. From that high point they could guide their shell-fire towards the British. So it was the British who fired back and ended up demolishing the tower and bringing the Virgin Mary down to Earth. The Germans were happy.

HAH! *OUR* SUPERSTITION IS THAT WHOEVER KNOCKS THE STATUE DOWN WILL *LOSE* THE WAR, BYE-BYE BRITS!

And, would you believe it? The war ended shortly after ... but with the defeat of Germany.

I TOLD YOU SO!

Funny fact: After the British knocked the statue down, it disappeared – probably sent to Germany to be melted down and turned into weapons.

When the war finished, Albert and its church were rebuilt. An exact copy of the statue stands there now. But it was suggested that the statue should be put back in her famous wartime pose! The people of Albert said, '*Non!*'

Simple spymen

Some places were haunted long before the First World War. But the war brought them new horrors and new ghosts. Take the ancient Tower of London, for example. The war brought it back into use in a horrible historical way…

Terror in the Tower

'Have you any last requests?' the Major asked the young man in the shabby black suit.

'I have, good sir. I would like to play my violin one last time. Before you shoot me.'

The Major nodded and opened a hatch in the steel door and called to the guard outside, 'Bring Herr Buschmann's violin from the office.' He turned back to the prisoner. 'You are honoured, young Fernando. You will be the first

60

to be executed in the Tower of London for hundreds of years.'

The young man gave a faint smile. 'It is a greater honour to die for Germany,' he said.

'It would be better to *live*,' the Major pointed out and pulled a wooden chair to the side of the bed and sat facing the German spy.

'My wife and child will suffer back in Germany. I regret being caught … but I do not regret spying for my country,' he said calmly.

The Major shook his head sadly. 'It was Germany that sent you here to die.'

'No, they sent me here to *spy*.'

'But they prepared you so badly we were *bound* to catch you!' the Major groaned. 'Don't you see that?'

'No,' the prisoner frowned.

The officer leaned forward and lowered his voice.

'You will die at dawn, so there is nothing to lose by telling you this, Fernando. But they trained you in the spy school at Rotterdam. The head of the spy school is Herr Flores.'

'Perhaps.'

'We *know* it is!' the Major sighed. 'And he sent you here with a passport written in his own handwriting. We recognized it at once.'

For the first time a small frown of uncertainty crossed the young German's face. The Major went on. 'He sent you to a hotel in the Strand where he sends *all* of his secret agents. He gave you a cover story – you were to say you were a salesman of cheese, bananas, safety-razors and potatoes ... but you know hardly anything about those things!'

The spy lowered his head a little in an admission of defeat. 'I sent in reports the best I could,' he muttered.

'You sent in reports that said we switch on London searchlights at 8 p.m. and switch them off again at 10:30 if no Zeppelins appear,' the officer said. 'That is no great secret to die for.'

'You know what messages I sent?'

'Of course! You sent the messages in code to a schoolmaster in Holland. That schoolmaster is a *British* spy. You were an amateur, Fernando. *We* will shoot you ... but it is *your* spy-masters who sent you to your death.'

There was a rap on the door and a guard handed a violin to the Major who passed it across to Fernando Buschmann.

For the next three hours, the sweet, mournful tones echoed round the ancient walls and stirred the ghosts of long-dead prisoners.

Slowly, the sky lightened through the barred window and hobnailed footsteps clattered in the corridor outside. The prisoner played one last melody but now the notes were wavering and disconnected. 'Nice tune,' the Major said.

'It's Pagliacci,' the German said. 'The music tells the story of a broken-hearted clown. Maybe that's all I was, Major.' He raised the violin to his lips and kissed it. 'Goodbye, I shall not want you any more.' He laid his precious instrument on the hard bed, straightened his back and faced the men who waited at the door. 'I am ready,' he said.

Fernando Buschmann faced an eight-man firing squad on the morning of 19 October 1915. He refused a blindfold, saying he wanted to die like a gentleman. He was one of 11 bungling, amateur German spies to die in the Tower during the First World War. A 12th was hanged at Wandsworth Prison.

On 13 November 1997, the papers connected with the case were sold at an auction in London.

The saddest was the letter from his wife to his lawyer Henry Garrett that read…

Dear Mr Garrett
         I would be grateful if you could send me details of my husband's last moments. Was he at least allowed to keep his violin till his last hours? Had he much to suffer? Will I find his tomb in London to weep at it? My only wish is to visit and to sleep there where my beloved husband is sleeping…

There were many ways to die, and many wasted lives, in the First World War. Fernando Buschmann's was just another one.

Awful agents

In the years before the First World War, Britain was overrun with German spies because they guessed this war would come one day. It wasn't 'til 1908 that Britain had any spy-catchers – the Secret Service Bureau.[1] Captain Vernon Kell was the only member of the Secret Service Bureau and by the start of the war in 1914 he had only nine officers. The Bureau did such a good job that they arrested 21 agents as soon as the war began.

1 In 1916, this was renamed Military Department 5 – the famous MI5. By the end of the war it had 844 members.

67

The Bureau had a lot of help from the German spies who were not too clever. In fact, they were awful agents. They got their information from Germans working in Britain – hairdressers and pub landlords were favourites because they heard lots of gossip. And German teachers were a bit treacherous, too! (Would you trust a teacher?)

Their code words included...

eggs = foot-soldiers

condensed milk = horse soldiers

margarine = guns

Dutch cheese = battleships

tinned lobster = torpedo boats

Now that code may be hard to crack (except 'eggs' which are easy to crack) but you don't have to be James Bond to solve the following genuine German code. Match the code to the real meaning ... the simple spymen left enough clues in the choice of words!

1 Floating down   a) Dartmouth Naval Base

2 Old folks at home   b) Destroyers

3 Dark melodies   c) Old battleships

4 Chattanooga Rag   d) Southampton

5 Down South   e) Submarines

6 Pirates of Penzance   f) Chatham Base

Answers

1e), 2c), 3a), 4f), 5d), 6b). How did you score?

Down South = Southampton! Chattanooga = Chatham. Difficult, eh? If you scored six out of six the good news is you'd make a spy. The bad news is it's a German spy. You'd be arrested and spend the war in jail – if you weren't shot.

That was too easy. So try this quick quiz…

Sly spy

Which of the following statements are true?

1 MI5 agents used girl guides to carry their messages

… but the girls had to promise not to read them.

2 An American (spying for Germany) was arrested as soon as his socks were tested. When they were soaked in water they produced invisible ink.

3 A German spy put up a poster in Portsmouth offering five pounds to anyone who would give him information about the warships there.

4 British spies in Germany were told, 'If someone starts taking an interest in you then you will end up having to kill him. So don't waste time. Do it.'

Answers

The above statements are all totally ridiculous. And they are all totally *true*. Girl guides *were* used to carry messages (because they proved more reliable than boy scouts!) and Brit agents in Germany really were 'licensed to kill'. In November 1997, MI5 published the secret files at last and these wacky facts came to light.

1916 – The Year of the Somme

In 1914, millions of men had rushed to join their armies and fight for their countries. By 1916, they are trained and ready to be sent off to fight the biggest battle ever. The battleground is around the River Somme in northern France.

This is to be the battle that ends the war for good! All it does is end the war for the million or so captured, wounded or killed. For the rest it goes on … and on and on…

Timeline 1916
25 January

'Conscription' comes to Britain. That means fit, single men *have* to join the army whether they like it or not.

February

The French and Germans begin the longest battle of the war, at the fortress of Verdun in north-eastern France. Even Big Bertha (that's a gun firing one-ton shells, not a woman) can't win it for the Germans.

March

German soldiers are told to have one day a week without food to save on supplies … but the officers seem to eat well *every* day!

24 April

The Irish rebel against British rule and try to seize Dublin *Post Office*! Brits soon *stamp* that out!

May

The only great sea battle of the war takes place at Jutland. Germans claim victory but never try to fight the Brit navy again.

5 June

Lord Kitchener's face is on a million posters saying 'Your country needs YOU!' Today he dies when his ship hits a mine.[1]

YOUR COUNTRY

NEEDS YOU

BUT I NEED A LIFEBOAT

---

1 In 1930, a German spy-master said that *he* arranged to have Kitchener killed. He claimed he got Irish enemies of Britain to sneak a bomb on board Kitchener's ship, then he watched from the shore as the bomb was detonated. Don't believe him. It was a mine!

1 July

The Battle of the Somme begins. Today Brits outnumber Germans seven to one … but lose seven men to every one German. Very bloody draw.

10 August

A frightful news film, *The Battle of the Somme*, is shown in Brit cinemas even though it's not over yet. It's seen by 20 million shocked Brits.

15 September

New Brit super-weapon, the 'Willie', enters the war. Luckily someone has changed its name to the 'Tank', giving rise to a horrible historical joke. Question: There were two flies in an airing cupboard. Which one was in the army? Answer: The one on the tank.

October

In a Brit election, the 'Peace' candidate is heavily defeated by the one supporting the war. For all the bloodshed, Brits back home still don't want peace.

14 November

End of the Battle of the Somme. Allied and German losses – over 1.3 million men. Allied gains – six miles. That's 120 men for every metre of ground won. Expensive ground.

WHERE'S THE REST OF THE ARMY?

YOU'RE LYING ON THEM

7 December

Lloyd George becomes new Brit prime minister. Old prime minister Asquith says, 'I distrust him.'

Silly (but true) story

In the great Somme advance of 1 July 1916, a soldier was given the job of taking a messenger pigeon in a basket to the front. He was told that an officer would use it to send a message when the first target was reached.

Back at headquarters, they waited hours and hours for the pigeon and finally it appeared. The anxious commander cried, 'Give me the message!' and it was handed to him.

He opened it and read, 'I am absolutely fed up with carrying this bloody bird around France.'

Daft DORA

Who was DORA? DORA was Britain's Defence of the Realm Act. And DORA could be *very* fussy.

The people of Britain had to live by DORA's rules. But which rules? Here are some strange regulations. But which are real DORA rules and which are real daft rules?

DEFENCE OF THE REALM ACT

YOU MUST NOT

1... loiter under a railway bridge
2... send a letter overseas written in invisible ink
3... buy binoculars without official permission
4... fly a kite that could be used for signalling
5... speak in a foreign language on the telephone
6... ring church bells after sundown
7... whistle in the street after 10 p.m. for a taxi
8... travel alone in a railway carriage over the Forth Bridge
9... push a handcart through the streets at night without showing a red light at the back and a white light on the front
10... eat sweets in the classroom

Answers

Numbers 1 to 9 are all DORA rules. (Only number 10 was not mentioned ... though some sneaky teachers probably tried to add it!)

One rule that upset children was the one that said, 'You must not keep fragments of Zeppelins or bombs as souvenirs'. All children hunted for these and ignored the law.

What's a Zeppelin? A huge German airship that flew over Britain and dropped bombs on cities. No one in Britain had ever suffered this sort of attack before and some people feared the dangers a bit too much.

Zeppelin Zep-panic

DORA ordered that no lights could be shown after dark. In 1916, in York, the first person fined was Jim Richardson, who was fined five shillings (25p) for lighting a cigarette in the street at night. The Zep-panicking magistrate told him that a lighted match could be seen by a Zeppelin flying 2,000 feet up.

The Rev Patrick Shaw was arrested for showing a light from his church, despite his plea that it was only a 'dim religious light'. The Zep-panicking magistrate fined him anyway.

Police also banned loud noises. In York, the Chief Constable told residents…

Do not laugh in the street, stop your dogs barking and do not bang doors because all these noises can be heard from a Zeppelin listening for its target.

The man was clearly a Yorkshire *pudding*! But was he any worse than the newspaper that had the bright idea to light a huge area of empty countryside at night to attract Zeppelins and then destroy them – like moths around a candle flame!

Foul food and worse water

If you think school dinners are bad, then you should be glad you didn't live in Europe in 1914–18. It's hard to tell if the food and drink was worse at home or in the army.

Would you like a cup of tea in the trenches? Or would you prefer a drink of milk in your wartime home?

You'd like tea in the trenches? Well, the soldiers' water had chloride of lime added to kill the germs in it. The trouble was the chloride of lime made the water taste *terrible*, even when it was boiled and used to make a cup of tea. It's a bit like drinking your local swimming-bath water. Yeuchy.

So, would you prefer…

Milk at home? In London, William Saxby, a milkman, was sentenced in 1917 to two months' hard labour for selling his customers milk watered down with 'foul water obtained from a public lavatory basin'. Yeuchier!

Rotten rations

British soldiers were offered a delightful tinned stew called Maconochie. A joke recipe appeared in a soldiers' newspaper. Sadly, it was close to the truth!

Maconochie Hotpot

1 Open one tin of Maconochie rations.
2 Warm gently until the greasy oil floats to the top. Remove this by blotting it up with a piece of flannel. (Place this on one side for later use.)
3 Remove the black lumps from the tin. These are potatoes.
4 Squeeze the greasy oil from the flannel into a frying-pan and gently fry the potatoes.
5 Take two handfuls of dried vegetables (they look like any other dead leaves). Mix with water flavoured with chloride of lime and pat into a pancake. This should be gently fried after the potatoes.
6 Heat up the remains of the stew, then serve with the potatoes and vegetables on a cold enamel plate.

Soldiers were also given bully beef (like corned beef) to which they liked to add raw onions. Sometimes they had to eat this with hard biscuits.

The French peasants who gave rooms to British soldiers were glad of these biscuits … they made excellent fire-lighters!

Jam was usually plum and apple and arrived in the trenches in tins. Empty tins made useful home-made grenades!

Young soldiers suffered badly. Ernest Parker, a soldier in the 10th Battalion of the Durham Light Infantry, said…

Army food was monotonous and in the trenches bully beef and bread, often without butter or jam, was the usual fare. Teenagers like myself were always hungry. Alas, when we needed food most it sometimes did not arrive at all, and it was far from pleasant to spend 24 hours or more in the front line with nothing to eat. Sometimes when drinking water did not arrive, we were driven to boiling water from shell holes and this may account for the crop of boils and diarrhoea that plagued us.

Apart from the bully beef and the Maconochie, the soldiers had two other big food complaints…

One was the cakes that friends and family sent from home! Deadlier than a German bullet, some soldiers reckoned.

The other pet hate was mentioned earlier. It featured in a popular poem of the time…

Fear

A terror hangs over our heads,
I scarcely dare to think
Of the awful doom that each one dreads
From which the bravest shrink.
It's not the crashing shrapnel shell,
It's not the sniper's shot,
It's not the machine-gun's burst of Hell,
These matter not a jot.
It's a far worse thing than that, son,
With which we have to grapple.
It's if we see another one
More tin of Plum and Apple.

Horse sense

The Allied soldiers complained but it was even worse for the German army. One tip sent to the soldiers read...

```
For tender roast horse flesh, you should
          boil it first in a little
             water, before you put it
                in the roasting pan.
```

But they only ate horses for the *mane* course.

Suffering civilians

British people may have gone hungry from time to time. But the people of Germany were starving for most of the First World War.

As early as 1915, 'Eat less' posters appeared all over Germany with the 'Ten food commandments'. These included…

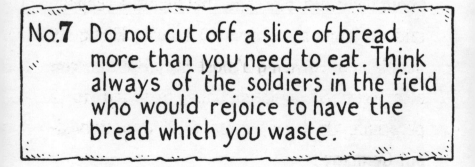

No.7 Do not cut off a slice of bread more than you need to eat. Think always of the soldiers in the field who would rejoice to have the bread which you waste.

Belly laughs

The British people believed that the Germans would be starved into defeat. In 1914, Germany only produced 80% of its food, 20% had to be imported, so the blockade of Germany by the Royal Navy caused severe shortages and suffering.

By the end of the war Germans were starving, but in September 1915, they could still laugh about the British blockade. That month a Zeppelin raid on London dropped 70 bombs, killing 26 people and wounding almost 100. But the crew also dropped a ham bone attached to a parachute. On it was written, 'A gift from starved-out Germany'.

By September 1918, the German people had stopped laughing … and they didn't have spare ham bones for jokes.

Hunger horrors

We all know what it's like to be hungry, but very few of us in Europe today know what it's like to be *really* starving, year after year.

Maybe you could try this diet for just *one day* and see how it feels. (Get your friends to sponsor you and give the money to a good cause.) Then remember this is how most Germans ate in the winter of 1916–17 on a *good* day. It was known as the Turnip Winter because turnip was the only food that was plentiful.

94

The Turnip Winter diet

You need:
six slices of bread
50g of meat
two teaspoons of sugar
two teaspoons of coffee
50g of cheese
one cup of soup
vegetables (half a turnip, handful
of peas, beans, mushrooms, nuts), half
a cup of blackberries

Breakfast
Two slices of bread (no butter), one cup
of coffee with a spoonful of sugar but
no milk
Lunch
Soup with meat and turnip chopped in,
peas and beans added. Cup of coffee, two
slices of bread
Supper
Cheese, two slices of bread, water
Snacks
Nuts and berries

And, now, the *bad* news…

• You would only have the mushrooms, nuts and berries if you'd gone out and picked them in the autumn. (You might have to fight the squirrels for the juicy ones!)

• The meat would probably be horse or dog. (After a day of the Turnip Winter diet you may look at your pet poodle and lick your lips.) Even the kangaroos in the German zoos were killed and eaten.

• You might not even be able to get dog meat. In April 1916, all Berlin butchers were closed for five days because they had no supplies of anything. In July 1916, women demonstrated outside the Town Hall in Dusseldorf demanding more meat and potatoes. When the Mayor offered them more beans and peas, they rioted and smashed every window in the Town Hall.

• Cream was only obtainable on a doctor's prescription.

• The German newspapers tried to calm things down – one published a long article proving that overeating was the cause of baldness!

• By late 1916, women queued outside food shops all night, bringing camp stools, knitting, etc. (One woman was seen in a queue with a sewing machine to pass the time.)

But by 1916 it wasn't only the Brits who hated the Kaiser. The Germans were beginning to turn against him. And no wonder. If food was bad in Britain it was worse in Germany…

Fake food

All Germans who lived through the First World War remembered not only the lack of food but the frightful food *substitutes* that they were forced to eat – known as 'ersatz' food. As the war dragged on, exhibitions were held all over Germany to demonstrate the huge range of ersatz food and drinks, for example…

Bread soon contained flour made from beans and peas, and often sawdust was added.

Cakes were made from clover and chestnut flour.

Meat was replaced by the rice lamb chop or the vegetable steak (pale green, made from spinach, spuds, ground nuts and eggs substitute).

Butter was 'stretched' with starch or made from a mix of curdled milk, sugar and yellow colouring.

Eggs were made from a mix of maize and potatoes.

Pepper was 'stretched' with ashes.

Fats were made – or attempted to be made – from rats, mice, hamsters, crows, cockroaches, snails, worms, hair clippings, old leather boots and shoes. None of those was very successful.

 Coffee was first made from roast nuts flavoured with coal tar – with sugar this was OK! Later came coffee-ersatz-ersatz – roasted acorns or beech nuts. Later still, when all acorns had to be fed to pigs, came coffee made from carrots and turnips.

Hungry people lose the will to fight. Germans lost that will – the Allies, who hadn't suffered nearly so much, did not lose their will. It's one of the reasons the Germans lost. It was also a reason why the Germans felt so bitter at losing. All that pain for nothing. Ten years after the First World War ended that bitterness drove them to support Adolf Hitler and a second war.

1917 – The Year of the Mud

The winter of 1916–17 is bitterly cold, but especially for the French. The Germans hold the north-west where most French coal mines are. One jeweller in Paris places a small lump of coal surrounded by diamonds in his window.

Houses in Paris are allowed only one electric light in each room (anyone caught with more will have their electricity cut off for three weeks!).

In Germany, coal is just as short. Berlin lights are to be put out by 9 p.m. Elephants from the circus are used in Berlin to pull coal carts from the railway stations – it saves wasting coal on steam trains or using horses that could be working in the army. German workers go on strike while French soldiers have their own rebellion. Everyone is desperate for peace – but the war goes on ... and on.

Timeline 1917
January
A munitions factory blows up in Silvertown, East London, killing 69.

February
The Russian people rebel against their leaders and Russian soldiers lend their rifles to help the revolution. Good news for Germany.

TROTSKY OVER HERE AND LENIN US A HAND

March

In Britain the Women's Army Auxiliary Corps (WAAC) is founded and a new joke is born...

April

The Doughboys are here! No, not bakers' men, but American soldiers as the USA joins the war. Meanwhile French troops rebel against their conditions.

May

UK horse-racing is stopped, followed by county cricket and league football.

June

Brit ban on rice being thrown at weddings and feeding birds – food is too precious.

July

The war now costs Britain nearly £6 million a day. Will they run out of money or men first?

I August

Terrific rain storms as the British attack in Flanders. The mud is as deadly an enemy as the Germans.

4 September

German submarines shell Scarborough. Why shell a seaside holiday town when it has a beach full of shells?

October

Brit bakers allowed to add potato flour to bread, while French bread has become grey, soggy stuff.

November

War between Russia and Germany coming to an end as the Russian 'Bolsheviks' start to take over their country.

6 December

German Giants reach London. (They're bomber aircraft, not monster men.) They're harder to catch than the old Zeppelins.

Wild Western Front

From November 1914 the two huge armies dug trenches in the ground and faced one another in a line from Belgium to Switzerland. From time to time one tried to attack and push back the other. The defenders usually won in the end ... but only after both sides had lost large numbers of men.

Lots of books have described trench life on the Western Front. The soldier's only comfort was that it was just as bad for the enemy as it was for himself. Here are six descriptions of trench life from Allied or Central Power soldiers. But which are which?

1 Which side suffered disgusting trenches?

Lice, rats, barbed wire, fleas, shells, bombs, underground caves, corpses, blood, liquor, mice, cats, filth, bullets, fire, steel; that is what war is. It is the work of the devil.

2 Which side fought 'til they were exhausted skeletons?

There were about 20 men. They walked like living plaster statues. Their faces stared at us like those of shrunken mummies, and their eyes seemed so huge that one saw nothing but eyes. Those eyes, which had not seen sleep for four days and nights showed the vision of death. Was this the dream of glory that I had when I volunteered to fight?

3 Which side fought because they thought it was their duty to God and that he was on their side?

Dear Parents

I am lying on the battlefield wounded in the body. I think I am dying. I am glad to have time to prepare for the heavenly home-coming. Thank you, dear parents God be with you.

4 Which side believed that its heavy shells would destroy the enemy trenches so all they had to do was walk across no man's land and take over?

For some reason nothing seemed to happen to us at first. We strolled along as though walking in the park. Then, suddenly, we were in the midst of a storm of machine-gun bullets and I saw men beginning to twirl round and fall in all kinds of curious ways as they were hit – quite unlike the way actors do it in films.

5 Which side sometimes shot the enemy as a sport?

We did some sniping. I had a very good corporal who was an excellent shot. He and I had a shooting competition. We took turns at the enemy in front of us while they were running about and moving around from time to time. That kept our troops amused and took their minds off the mud that was up to their knees.

Answers

Of course, if you guessed right then it would be *luck*. Because any of these could have been written by Allied or Central Power soldiers. Life was miserable whichever side you fought for.

1 German painter, Otto Dix.

2 German soldier, Wilhelm Hermanns.

3 German student, 24-year-old Johannes Haas.

4 British soldier, Private W Slater.

5 British Captain Goving.

Terrible toilets

A German writer described the pleasures of being out of the front line. What would you do to relax? Sleep? Write letters to your family? Clean your toenails? Not Erich Maria Remarque, the author of a famous book, *All Quiet on the Western Front,* who said that...

The experienced soldiers don't use the unpleasant, indoor, common toilet, where 20 men sit side by side in a line. As it is not raining, they use the individual square wooden boxes with carrying handles on the sides. They pull three into a circle and sit there in the sun all afternoon, reading, smoking, talking, playing cards.

In the front-line trenches it was different and more dangerous. There were no toilets in the Brit trenches, just buckets. If you upset the sergeant you would be given the job of taking the buckets out after dark. Your job was to dig a hole and empty the buckets. Once you were out of the cover of the trenches, you were in danger, but some soldiers still lit cigarettes to hide the smell from the buckets. Enemy snipers were just waiting to aim at the glow of a cigarette end. Emptying toilet buckets could be bad for your health.

Even *going* to the toilet shed just behind the trenches was dangerous. The enemy knew men used these toilets at dawn and liked to drop a few shells among the toilet huts to catch the soldiers with their pants down!

Terrible toilet tale 1...

A major found some deserted houses for his men. He looked at the sign at the end of the street and copied it carefully. Then he sent a message to his soldiers...

You will find rooms in "Verbod te wateren"

Unfortunately, he couldn't read Flemish and didn't understand that the sign wasn't the street name. It was a warning notice that said, 'You must not pee in the street'.

Terrible toilet tale 2...

Army boots had to be tough. The trouble was the leather was so hard it gave men blisters. Old soldiers knew the answer...

You probably won't want to try this with your new school shoes. But, if you do, remember to *empty* them before you put them on!

Terrible toilet tale 3...

In the 1917 battles in Flanders, the troops didn't have properly built trenches, just shell holes protected by sandbags. And there were certainly no toilet huts. One officer complained...

If you wanted to do your daily job of urinating and otherwise there was an empty bully-beef tin, and you had to do that in front of all your men, and then chuck the contents (but not the bully-beef tin) out over the back.

He forgot to mention one important thing. Find out which way the wind is blowing first!

Frightful fun and gruesome games

If you grew bored with 'chatting' you could always try one of the violent entertainments that soldiers used to pass the time…

Games you wouldn't want to play

1 Free the prisoner (Australian Rules)

To play:
- a grenade
- a German prisoner.

The rules:

First find a prisoner who wants to go free. Take him to the gates of the prison and place a hand grenade in his back pocket. Pull the pin out of the grenade (which will explode in five seconds). Hold the prisoner for a count of 'One – two', then release him and tell him to run. If he gets the grenade out of his pocket in the remaining three seconds, he is the winner and is free to go. If he gets the grenade out of his pocket and throws it back at you, then you are the losers. But that's the risk you take.

There are reports of this happening, so it is probably true, but extremely rare.

2 Beetle racing

You need:

- two or more beetles
- a table
- sugar
- matchsticks.

To play:

Each 'jockey' chooses a beetle and holds it at one end of the table. A sugar lump is placed at the other end of the table to attract the beetles. Every jockey places one matchstick on the table. On a signal, the beetles are released. The first beetle to reach the sugar wins and the winning jockey collects everyone else's matchsticks. (And the beetles get to eat the sugar.)

I'M A WOOD BEETLE.
I'D RATHER EAT
THE MATCHSTICK

3 Sea swimming

You need:

• the sea.

To play:

At Gallipoli the chief hobby for Anzac troops was swimming. This took a lot of courage because the Turkish army were shelling the beaches. Troops swam for fun and to keep cool (but also because there was no water for washing in the trenches). Beaches were somewhat spoilt by the sight and smell of dead horses, mules and donkeys.

IT'S STILL BETTER THAN AN ENGLISH BEACH

4 Barge boating

You need:

• a wooden box

• two shovels.

In 1917, as Sergeant Ernest Parker was sitting reading at the entrance to his dugout in the banks of the Yser canal, he saw an exciting regatta…

Lustily plying two oars, a ruffian member of my band was propelling a rectangular box up and down the canal. Shovels were the oars and when rival craft were launched a naval battle began, cheered by the spectators, who were hoping that somebody would take a plunge into the black slime of the canal.

Weird words

If you were a British soldier in the First World War, you would soon learn a new language – army slang. In fact, there were *two* languages to learn – one used by the officers and one by the ordinary soldiers.

Could you learn to 'sling the bat' (speak in the local language, that is) with the soldiers or the officers?

Batty bat slinging

What would you do if someone came up to you and said...

Of course, that will all make perfect sense to you. No? Oh, well, here's an explanation…

1 I'd love some nice meat pudding followed by bread and cheese, washed down with a cup of strong tea. For afters I'd like jam on bread.

2 Now, my good man, this afternoon (p.m.) we need some tidying up before the mad army chaplain comes to inspect our sleeping bags.

3 I received a wound that will get me sent home when a mortar bomb, a mine and another mortar bomb landed in my dugout.

4 I am itching from all the lice in my shaggy fur coat and I wish I was back in my normal street clothes.

124

Sometimes the soldiers cheered themselves up by making fun of official army language. Their daily ration of spirits was 'service rum, diluted' – SRD. But the sergeant who served it out tended to get to a trench and say, 'I'll have mine with you,' and pour himself a tot.

He did the same in every trench. If you were unlucky enough to be in the last trench, then there was no rum and a very drunk sergeant. So what did SRD stand for? 'Seldom reaches destination'!

And the Royal Army Medical Corps (RAMC) became the 'rob all my comrades' because soldiers suspected medical staff went through the pockets of the wounded men.

The same RAMC would sometimes be unsure what was wrong with a patient, so they labelled him 'not yet diagnosed' (NYD). Soldiers swore the letters stood for 'not yet dead'.

Esses Ink Gee Nuts Ack London – Toc Ack London King!

No, that isn't a secret code to *disguise* the meaning of messages. It's a way of making messages quite *clear* over a crackling phone line. So 'Harry – Edward – London – London – Oranges' is 'Hello'. Learn the list, impress your friends and confuse your teacher with the Great War code...

A = Ack	J = Johnnie	S = Esses
B = Beer	K = King	T = Toc
C = Charlie	L = London	U = Uncle
D = Don	M = Emma	V = Vic
E = Edward	N = Nuts	W = William
F = Freddie	O = Oranges	X = X-ray
G = Gee	P = Pip	Y = Yorker
H = Harry	Q = Queen	Z = Zebra
I = Ink	R = Robert	

Nutty names

Any names in the language of the enemy were suddenly unpopular.

France has a perfume called 'eau de Cologne' (water of Cologne), but Cologne is in Germany. They tried to change it to 'eau de Provence' because Provence is in France, but the idea never caught on.

The name changing went further in Germany. All bars, hotels and shops with English or French names were changed, causing great confusion.

In Breslau, the German military governor went to a sweet shop...

In 1915, Italy joined the war against Germany, and Berlin cafés stopped serving 'Italian salad'…

Jolly Germans

Even in the gloom of the war Germany kept its theatres open. But the plays were pretty miserable. The most popular one of 1917 was *Maria Magdalena* about life in a small town. Well, that's not quite true … it's more about *death* in a small town!

Which character would you like to be? Can you pick the *two* that stayed alive?

1 Mrs Magdalena – a hard-working and caring mum

2 Mr Magdalena – a hard-working and caring dad

3 Maria – their daughter, a beautiful and popular girl

4 The cat – the family's faithful, furry friend

5 Fritz – Maria's lover

6 Hans – a rival for the love of Maria

Want a clue? Of the four who die, one dies in a duel, one suffers a fit on stage, one puts a bullet through their brain and (best of all) one throws themselves down a well.

Answer

The mother dies of a fit on stage, Fritz is killed in a duel with Hans who commits suicide, so Maria jumps into a well. At the end, only the father and the family cat are still alive!

Ropey rhymes

Poetry from the First World War is still remembered and enjoyed today by millions of people. Quite rightly.

But there were also some popular rhymes that have been forgotten. The simple poems and songs that soldiers repeated to try and stay cheerful in the bad times. The *bad* news is that most of them are too rude to be printed – even in Horrible Histories!

But here are a few that you may enjoy.

(Hint: Dig a hole in your back garden, flood it with water and sit there for a few hours while your family throw pots, pans or pianos out of upstairs windows on to you. This will get you in the mood.)

1 This limerick was popular around 1915…

There was a young lady of Ypres
Who was hit in the cheek by two snipers.
The tunes that she played
Through the holes that they made
Beat the Argyll and Sutherland pipers.

2 Private Stanley Woodburn wrote his will on a postcard and carried it in his pocket. He wrote it as a poem…

My belongings I leave to my next of kin,
My purse is empty there's nothing in;
My uniform, rifle, my pack and kit,
I leave to the poor devil they will fit;
But if this war I manage to clear
I'll keep it myself for a souvenir.

Private Woodburn was killed in France in April 1918.

3 Charlie Chaplin, star of silent films, left his home in England in 1913. When the war started a year later, he did not return to join the army. Soldiers made up a popular song…

The moon shines bright on Charlie Chaplin,
His boots are cracking, for want of blacking.
And his little baggy trousers they want mending,
Before we send him to the Dardanelles…

Charlie didn't see the joke! 'I really thought they were coming to get me!' he said. 'It scared the daylights out of me.'

4 Many Brit soldiers had their own monthly magazines in the trenches. The poems they published were a bit of fun in the misery of the war…

There was a young Boche at Bazentin
Who liked the first trench that he went in.
But a 15 inch 'dud'
Sent him flat in the mud
And he found that his helmet was
bent in.

5 Not all of the poems were funny. There were some things that soldiers said over and over again to cheer themselves up. This simple poem in a trenches' magazine took three of the sayings as its first three lines, then added its own fourth line…

It's a long road that has no turning,
It's never too late to mend;
The darkest hour is before the dawn
And even this war must end.

6 Poems were used in the hate-war against the enemy. In a children's magazine there was one to warn of the dangers of German toys which, of course, were supposed to be poisonous!

Little girls and little boys,
Never suck your German toys;
German soldiers licked will make
Darling Baby's tummy ache.
Parents, you should always try
Only British toys to buy;
Though to pieces they be picked,
British soldiers can't be licked.

7 Soldiers were fond of singing. When they couldn't find a suitable song, they took a popular one and changed the words. In 1914, they were singing…

Though your heart may ache a while
… never mind.
Though your face may lose its smile
… never mind.
For there's sunshine after rain
And then gladness follows pain,
You'll be happy once again
… never mind.

The words were soon replaced by more bitter ones...

If you're hung up on barbed wire
… never mind.

Or…
If your sleeping place is damp
… never mind.
If you wake up with a cramp
… never mind.
If your trench should fall in some
Fill your ears and make you dumb
While the sergeant drinks your rum
… never mind.

8 Love songs became war songs…

If you were the only girl in the world,
And I were the only boy,
Nothing else would matter in the world today,
We would go on loving in the same old way.
A garden of Eden, just made for two…

Became…

If you were the only Boche in the trench,
And I had the only bomb,
Nothing else would matter in the world that day,
I would blow you up into eternity.
A Chamber of Horrors, just made for two…

9 Even religious songs were made fun of, 'What a Friend we Have in Jesus' became…

When this lousy war is over, oh how happy I will be,
When I get my civvy clothes on, no more soldiering for me.
No more church parades on Sunday,
No more putting in for leave.
I will kiss the sergeant major,
How I'll miss him, how I'll grieve.

(The word 'lousy' in the first line was often replaced by a ruder word.)

10 But the song that summed up the First World War the best was the simplest one of all. It was sung to the tune of 'Auld Lang Syne' (the one tipsy parents join hands to sing at New Year and embarrass you with).

We're here because we're here because
We're here because we're here.
We're here because we're here because
We're here because we're here.

Says it all really.

Horrible historical joke

The soldiers in the front line enjoyed a joke, even in the terror of the trenches. They produced their own magazines and their jokes were often about the senior officers who were miles behind the lines when the shooting started.

One popular cartoon was this one...

Major-General (addressing the men before practising an attack in the training camp behind the lines). 'I WANT YOU TO UNDERSTAND THAT THERE IS A DIFFERENCE BETWEEN A REHEARSAL AND THE REAL THING. THERE ARE THREE ESSENTIAL DIFFERENCES. FIRST, THE ABSENCE OF THE ENEMY. NOW (turning to the Sergeant Major), WHAT IS THE SECOND DIFFERENCE?

Sergeant Major. 'THE ABSENCE OF THE GENERAL, SIR.'

Painful punishments

An army, like a school, needs discipline. Men have to learn to obey orders or else. Or else what? There were various punishments that your teachers might like to adopt for your school … so keep this page out of their sight.

Field punishment No. 1

In this notorious Brit punishment, the offender is lashed, or crucified, to a gun wheel, tied by wrists and ankles for one hour in the morning and one in the evening for up to 21 days. The intention is to humiliate the soldier. It was rumoured that soldiers were lashed to guns in action.

Toothbrush torture

The Germans had their own way of dealing with problem soldiers. Troublemakers in training were…

• made to scrub out the corporals' room with a toothbrush.

• made to clear the barrack square of snow with hand-brushes and dustpans.

On Sundays (the recruits' only day off) they could be…

• forced to parade in full uniform with pack and rifle and then practise attacking and lying down in a muddy field until exhausted and filthy…

• ...then, four hours later, made to report with every item of uniform and kit cleaned, hands bleeding and raw from the cleaning.

Once those trained men were sent to the front, they were given a bunch of flowers to wear in their belts.

False fable

Many British soldiers believed that German soldiers were tied to their machine-guns to stop them from running away. In fact, German machine-gunners wore special belts with which they could carry their machine-guns and leave their hands free. If these soldiers were killed while carrying their gun, British soldiers would find the bodies 'tied' to the guns.

Cruel court martials

If a soldier was accused of a serious crime – like dropping his weapon and running away, or shooting himself in the foot to avoid going into battle – he'd be given a trial, known in the army as a 'court martial'.

Could you be a judge? Try these cases…

The case of Bellwarde Ridge

Private Allen and Private Burden were in the same regiment.

In June 1915, their regiment was ordered to move forward to the Bellwarde Ridge, France, which the Germans were defending furiously. Private Peter Allen didn't fancy walking towards machine-guns, so he took his rifle and shot himself in the leg. He was sent to hospital to recover and then ordered to serve two years in prison with hard labour.

Private Herbert Burden had joined up the year before. He told the recruiting officer he was 18 but he lied. He was just 16. When he was ordered to attack Bellwarde Ridge, he was just 17 – the age of many schoolboys today. The attack was a disaster and Herbert's friends died all around him. He had done his best but, in the end he turned and ran from the battlefield.

He was court-martialled and found guilty. What would you do with Herbert? Remember what had

happened to Peter Allen – who didn't even get to the fight. Remember that Herbert was only a boy. And remember that he'd been under heavy fire.

a) Give him a short rest then send him back into battle.

b) Send him home because he had been too young when he joined the army.

c) Give him two years' hard labour, the same as soldiers who wounded themselves.

d) Shoot him.

The case of king's crater

Sergeant Joe Tose and his officer, Lieutenant Mundy, left the safety of their trench to patrol a huge bomb crater in no man's land known as king's crater.

As they reached the crater, they were attacked by a larger patrol of German soldiers. Lieutenant Mundy was shot.

Sergeant Tose ran back to the trench and decided to warn the rest of his battalion. To slow down the German attackers, he jammed his rifle across the trench and set off for the rear trenches. As he had no weapon, he was charged with 'casting away his weapon in the face of the enemy'.

Everyone said that he was a good soldier. (One witness said that the Germans spoke good English and, to add to the confusion, had called out 'Retreat!') What would you do with Joseph Tose?

a) Give him a medal for his quick thinking in saving his patrol.

b) Take his sergeant's position from him and send him back to fight as a private.

c) Strap him to a gun carriage for two hours a day for 21 days as Field Punishment No. 1.

d) Shoot him.

Answers

In both cases the men were shot. Men who avoided battle by shooting themselves were not executed. Herbert Burden was one of three 17-year-olds who were shot by the British in the First World War.

Sergeant Tose was disgraced and forgotten. He did not even get his name on his village war memorial until his case was looked at 80 years later. His name was finally added in 1997.

In the First World War, the British shot 268 men for deserting their posts. (These are just two examples.) The German records were destroyed, but they must have had the same problems. Yet it seems they shot only 48 of their own men. The Russians gave up shooting their own soldiers and the Australians never shot one.

1918 - The Year of Exhaustion

The Allies and the Central Powers have been battering at one another's doors for over three years and are exhausted. The Germans have decided to make one huge attack before they starve to death.

It is like charging with a battering-ram at a rotten door. The Allies give way and are pushed back, and back and back. The Germans seem to be the winners!

But the Germans are rushing forward too quickly. Their supplies can't keep up with them and they soon run out. When the Allies stop and turn, the

Germans have nothing left to give. The Allies push on and on and on. All the way to Germany. The starved and feeble Germans are the losers … and all because they had been the winners.

Timeline 1918
January
Britain is forced to have two meatless days a week and no meat for breakfast. Shops with margarine are raided by desperate women!

25 February
Meat, butter and margarine rationed in the south of England and the queues (and the fighting shoppers) stop.

21 March

Called the 'last day of trench warfare'. The Germans break out and smash the Allies back from the trenches. Shells fall on Paris.

1 April

The Royal Air Force is formed and celebrates by shooting down German ace von Richthofen – the Red Baron – three weeks later.

May

The German government wants young people to marry before they are 20 to produce more children for the country (which is running short of people).

154

June

Thirty people die in Lancashire from Spanish flu. No one has any idea how many millions it's about to kill. Far more than the war, for sure.

18 July

At the River Marne, the Allies stop retreating. The tide is turning back towards Germany. The Russians massacre their royal family.

8 August

German General Ludendorff calls this 'the black day for the German army' as they are driven back. Still, no one expects the war to end this year.

29 September

Bulgarians have had enough and ask for peace. The beginning of the end for the Central Powers.

October

German sailors are ordered to make one great last voyage to destroy the Brit fleet – or be destroyed. Sailors refuse and pour water on their ships' boiler fires.

9 November

Kaiser Wilhelm is thrown out of Germany. He retires to Belgium. After what he did to them four years ago, it's not surprising they don't want him! He ends up in Holland.

11 November

Armistice Day and peace is agreed at last. The peace document is signed at the 11th hour of this 11th day of the 11th month.

PITY IT TOOK FOUR YEARS, FOUR MONTHS AND FOUR DAYS TO GET HERE

28 December

Women vote in Britain for the first time. War has changed something, anyway.

Suffering shock

The huge shells that exploded during a battle killed and wounded millions of soldiers. But they had another effect that no one saw and few people understood in 1914–18. It was the effect of days of endless noise and dreadful fear on men's minds.

Bombardments broke the minds of some men as surely as they broke the bodies of others.

The popular name for the effect was 'shell-shock' – the medical name is now 'post-traumatic stress disorder'. It doesn't matter what you call it really. Men suffered nightmares and fear of loud noises for the rest of their lives. It affected soldiers of all countries, during battles and long after them. In 1916, British Lieutenant Frederick Rees explained how shell-shock ruined a soldier's common sense...

Last night a man had an attack of nerves. He picked up a box of bombs, climbed out of the trench and threw them about in no man's land. He was lucky not to be shot. Either side would have shot him if he had come near when he still had those bombs. However, they got him back safe, poor chap.

Cruel for creatures

The animals that went to war didn't start the fight and didn't ask to go. But they were shot at and bombed and gassed and diseased as cruelly as their human masters. It was beastly being a beast in the First World War. If you're the sort of person who's pained by the thought of a pet with a prickle in its paw, it may be better to skip this section. If you enjoy raw hamster-burgers at school dinners, read on…

Creature cwiz

True or false?

1 In the First World War, British dogs were horses.

2 The best horses were saved for the army priests (the chaplains).

3 German soldiers wiped out a herd of rare European bison in Poland.

4 A British regiment made a miniature steel helmet for their pet dog.

5 The German army fitted their horses with gas masks.

6 A chick named Dick was used to detect enemy aircraft.

7 Goldfish were banned from battle areas because water was precious.

8 Horse droppings were used to make gas for heat and light.

9 Soldiers kept canaries because their song cheered everyone up.

10 The Allies won the war because they had a better supply of horses.

Answers

1 True. The British army supplied all the animals they needed but, to keep everything simple, they called these animals 'horses' ... even if they were guard dogs, oxen, reindeer or camels!

2 False. The chaplains were given horses at the start of the war but there was a shortage of horses for the fighting men. The chaplains had their horses taken from them and were given bicycles instead!

3 False. The herd of bison wiped out the Germans! The animals were grazing peacefully and ignoring the soldiers. Then a rifle was fired and the angry bison charged. They gored and trampled the German soldiers to death. Only 20 soldiers survived.

4 True. The dog was a stray that adopted the gunners. It became their lucky mascot. The death of the dog would have meant bad luck, so they protected it from 'stray' bullets and shells with a steel helmet.

5 True. The masks (which looked a bit like a nose-bag) didn't work very well and didn't protect the animals' eyes from the stinging gas. But at least the kindly Germans were *trying* to help their four-legged friends.

6 True. Driver David Spink rescued a half-starved chicken near St Quentin in 1918 and christened it Dick. When Allied aircraft flew over it was fine, but it dived for cover (and so did David Spink's company) when an enemy aircraft was overhead. After the war, Dick travelled back to Britain in Driver Spink's haversack and enjoyed a happy retirement.

7 False. Goldfish were very useful. After a gas attack, the gas helmets were rinsed with water. A goldfish was then dropped into the rinsing water. If the goldfish died then the mask was still poisoned and needed to be washed again. (Sadly, there is no record of a goldfish ever getting a medal for bravery.)

8 True. A horse produced about 14 or 15 kilograms of droppings every day. (Do you ever wonder who gets the job of measuring these things?)

The British alone had 870,000 horses in action by the end of the war. That is nearly 13 million kilos of horse muck being produced *every day*! Some was buried, some burned, some spread on fields as fertilizer. But some was heated to give off a gas that powered lamps and heaters. (Might it have been quicker just to put a lighted match to the horse's bum?)

9 False. Soldiers did keep canaries, but they were used in underground tunnels to check for gas. (If the bird fell off its perch, then there was gas down there.) Some of the bird handlers became very attached to their canaries and risked their own lives to save the birds during gas attacks. Why bother? They could always find another canary going cheap... Cheep! Cheep!

10 True. At least that's what British General Haig said after the war. 'If the Germans had a horse service as good as the British, then they would have won the war.'

Brave beasts

Men and women performed some incredibly brave acts in the face of the enemy. A German hero was covered in Iron Crosses, a British hero was covered in medals and an American hero, called Cher Ami, was covered in feathers. Because Cher Ami was a pigeon!

Duck, dove!

No, Cher Ami didn't fly over enemy forces and drop bombs on them, stupid. He carried a message from US soldiers in battle and saved dozens of lives. Imagine the sadness when he finally died...

U.S. TIMES

DOVE CONQUERS ALL

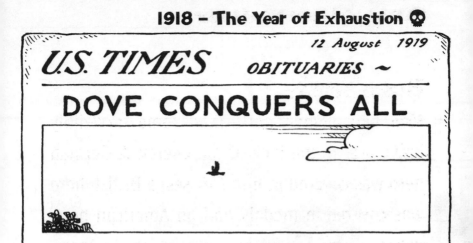

Cher Ami is dead. The pigeon that won the hearts of all true Americans has hopped the twig and passed peacefully away to that great pigeon loft in the sky.

It was just a year ago that Cher Ami flew to fame when he joined Major Charles Whittlesey's brigade. In the Argonne Forest, eastern France, the brigade found itself surrounded by enemy forces, starving and exhausted with many dead and wounded. Then shells began to land on the American survivors – but they were American shells aimed at them by mistake. There was only one way to get a message out of the deadly circle of machine-guns: a carrier pigeon.

Whittlesey scribbled a note: 'Our own forces are dropping shells on us! For heaven's sake stop it!' He took a pigeon from its basket but the frightened bird broke loose and flew for home – the US army

base camp. There was just one bird left – one last hope – a black cock called Cher Ami. Whittlesey clipped the message to the brave bird's leg and set it free. But Cher Ami flew up to the nearest tree and began preening its feathers. The brigade threw sticks and stones but still the perverse pigeon refused to budge. Finally Whittlesey climbed the tree and shook the branch. Cher Ami took the hint and set off for home.

The enemy saw at once that it was carrying a message and turned the full firepower of the forces towards it. One shot took off part of the battered bird's leg, passed through its chest and knocked out one eye. The peppered pigeon lost height, then, amazingly, recovered and flew on to deliver the message and the brigade was saved. 'Without that bird we'd have been wiped out, that is certain,' Whittlesey said. 'The 384 men who survived owed their lives to Cher Ami's courage.'

The heroic homing pigeon was patched up and brought back to a hero's welcome in America, where he died peacefully yesterday. He will be stuffed and go on display at the Smithsonian Institute.

Feathered fighters

1 Gallant pigeons like Cher Ami had another use. If soldiers became cut off from their supplies and were starving, they could always eat the birds!

2 Pigeon *pies* are very tasty, but pigeon *spies* were also valuable. Baskets full of British pigeons were dropped into French and Belgian villages that had been captured by the Germans. Villagers could then attach messages to the pigeons, which would fly back to Britain. The messages could tell the Allies what the enemy was up to. This is spying, of course, and the punishment for spying in war was to be shot. But it was even more dangerous being a pigeon. Sixteen thousand were dropped, but only one in ten returned.

3 The Germans took the problem of pigeon spies seriously. They cleverly planted baskets of German pigeons in the villages. Anyone who attached a message would see the bird fly off to Germany.

4 The Germans also formed squadrons of hawks and falcons to catch any pigeon flying over the English Channel back to Britain. This was rotten luck if you were an innocent pigeon on a day trip to Paris.

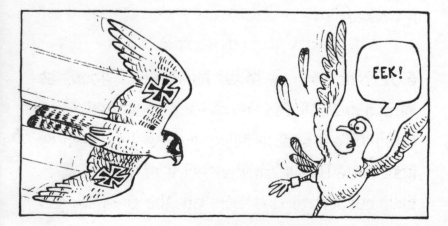

5 In the mud and rain of 1917, a group of soldiers was cut off and attached a message to a pigeon. The pigeon was too soaked to fly. It flopped into no man's land ... then started walking towards the German lines with its message! If the Germans knew the Brits were alone they would attack and finish them off! The Brits had to shoot the plodding pigeon. Their other bird was just as wet. One soldier suggested drying it in the dugout oven, but in the end the soldiers dried it by blowing on its feathers. It worked.

6 A French pigeon saved hundreds of troops at Verdun in 1916. The French were being shelled by Germans but had no heavy guns of their own to fight back. They wanted to get a message out to their gunners to say, 'Here are the German gun positions. Aim at them and stop them destroying us.' A greyhound got the message through, though he was wounded. And a pigeon got through just before it died of its wounds. The pigeon was given France's highest *human* medal for bravery – the *Legion d'Honneur*. The men and women who won the *Legion d'Honneur* must have been a bit annoyed by this! It's like saying, 'Here's your medal. Wear it with pride. You are as brave as a pigeon!'

The tale of a dog

Pigeons weren't the only courageous creatures to help their human masters in the First World War. There were dog heroes too. Heroes like Stubby the American pit bull terrier...

Stubby was a poor and homeless stray when Rob Conroy found him on the streets of Hartford, Connecticut. Nothing could separate these pals, not even the First World War. When Rob went to war, Stubby went with him.

Stubby was smuggled all the way to the war zone with the gallant guys in the 102nd Infantry Battalion. But he was no pampered pet, oh no! Stubby was a priceless guard dog with sharper eyes and ears than any sentry.

No matter what the enemy threw at him, Stubby ran out on to the battlefield and found the wounded. Then he lay beside them 'til the stretchers reached him. They called it no man's land, but it wasn't no dog's land!

And while the tired troopers slept, Stubby watched over them. One night he warned them of a gas attack. Another night a sneaking enemy soldier slipped into the US trenches — and left with Stubby's teeth in his butt!

Stubby fought in 17 battles. There was no way they could pin all his medals on his brave little chest — so they had a special blanket made. When the proud pooch met President Woodrow Wilson he wore it.

The First World War ended, but Stubby's work went on. He toured the country with Rob Conroy to raise money for victims of the fighting. What a courageous canine! Stubby! Man's best friend … ever!

Daring dogs

1 Dogs made useful messengers. They could be trained to run over the battlefield with messages fastened to their collars. Enemy soldiers watched for messenger dogs and tried to turn them into dead dogs.

2 Of course, the Germans had dogs just as brave as Stubby. One was used to carry secret messages backwards and forwards across the trenches. The German dog was the perfect spy courier. The British tried everything to capture him – nets and traps all failed – until the Allied soldiers came up with a devious dodge. They set a female dog to attract him into their hands. One wag of her tail and the German spy-dog was caught. (Let this be a lesson to you gentlemen readers … if a young lady wags her tail at you, *paws* before you run after her!)

3 Dogs were also put in harnesses and used to drag machine-guns around the battlefield. The Italian army used them to pull supply carts over the Alps. In the summer, this would have turned them into 'hot dogs', I guess.

4 Dogs also had reels of telephone cable strapped to their backs. As they ran along, they left a trail of cable behind them and linked the men in the trenches to the support troops behind them. Enemy gunners were always trying to cut these links and would shoot at cable layers. Dogs were faster than men, smaller and harder to hit than men, and it didn't matter so much if a dog was killed … unless you were the dog, of course.

5 When the war started, German shepherd dogs in Britain suddenly became unpopular – just because of their name! So the name was changed to 'Alsatian' and it's stayed that way ever since. (If you want to test your teacher, tell them of the German shepherd name-change, then say, 'What *other* creatures changed their English name in the First World War?' The answer is … the British royal family. They changed their family name from the German Saxe-Coburg-Gotha to Windsor. Like the Alsatians, they too are stuck with it.)

6 Some dogs went across to the enemy! No, they weren't traitors. Early in the war, French and German troops were in trenches just 30 metres apart. They sent each other friendly messages, newspapers and tobacco, tied to the dog's collar. One French corporal had left his wife behind in Germany when the war started. A dog brought him a message from her saying she was quite well and sent her love; the Germans passed it on by puppy post.

7 Terriers were useful for killing rats in the trenches. A devoted soldier wrote a poem to his dog, Jim…

Jim

A tough little, rough little beggar,
And merry the eyes on him.
But no German or Turk
Can do dirtier work
With an enemy rat than Jim.

And when the light's done
and night's falling,
And shadows are darkling and dim,
In my coat you will nuzzle
Your pink little muzzle
And growl in your dreams, little Jim.

There is no record of what the rats thought of little Jim.

Of course, not every company in the trenches had a rat-catcher like Jim. What did these poor soldiers do?

They tamed the rats and kept them as pets instead!

Rotten for rats

Rats enjoyed the First World War … mostly. There was always plenty to eat because the soldiers brought tons of supplies with them. But most soldiers hated the robbing rodents and spent a lot of their spare time trying to massacre the creepy creatures. Apart from shooting them in the open, they also tried some sneaky tricks. The following were all tried in the trenches with great success…

Vanquish Vile Vermin!

Method 1

1 If rats have been at your bread then place the ruined loaves on the floor of your dugout.

2 Find yourself a spade and torches. Switch out the lights.

3 When you hear the rats swarming over the bread then switch on the torches and smash the rats to a pulp.

184

Method 2

1 Place cordite at the entrance to rat holes and light it. The smoke will drive out the rats.

2 Wait by the exit and smash them with wooden clubs.

Method 3

1 Put a bayonet on the end of your rifle.

2 Put a piece of cheese on the end of the bayonet. Point it towards the enemy lines.

3 When a rat begins to nibble at the cheese, pull the trigger. You can't miss!

Horrible Histories health warning:
Cordite was used as an explosive to propel shells from guns. A group of Australian soldiers smoked out rats this way until the cordite came in contact with an unexploded German mine. Twenty men were injured ... but the rats were probably pulped!

Soldiers believed that rats knew when a bombardment was coming because the creatures would run away from the trenches that were in danger. They even believed that the biggest rats – usually nicknamed 'corpse rats' – could kill a cat or a dog.

German soldiers often kept cats in the front line, not simply to catch rats but because cats also gave early warning of a British gas attack. They became restless as though they could detect the poison gas in very low concentrations before the main cloud appeared.

Horrible historical joke

In June 1917, it was against British law to feed pigeons. This was part of the plan to save food. Not everyone agreed that this was a smart move.

In one of the soldiers' magazines, the following joke appeared...

A driver has been punished for giving his bread ration to his horse. He certainly deserved it. We are totally against cruelty to animals.

Women and children

The First World War affected women and children more than any other war had done. Before 1914, wars had been about men fighting men; women and children had been simply victims – they got themselves massacred if they were unlucky enough to be in a battle zone. They were starved and lost husbands and children, but they weren't seen as active participants in the war. That was about to change.

Wicked women

In July 1915, 30,000 women paraded in London under the banner, 'We demand the right to serve'. Women slowly began to take up jobs in war-work, especially making weapons and ammunition (munitions).

The miserable men didn't want women in the factories. They thought it would give the women a taste of freedom and change them. They were right! By the end of the war, British women could…

- smoke cigarettes openly
- drink in public houses
- openly use cosmetics
- swear
- wear short skirts and bras
- wear short hair (to control the nits)

- go to the cinemas without a man
- play football (factories started women's teams)
- then, Land Girls, who'd taken the jobs of farm labourers, began to wear their trousers off-duty!

In short, they started doing all the things men had been doing for years. (Oh, all right, you *didn't* see a lot of men in lipstick, short skirts and bras, but you know what I mean!). Many people were shocked by these changes. Now it would seem shocking for women *not* to be able to do all these things.

190

The German women worked just as hard but didn't earn the same sort of freedom. German men did not approve of freedom for their women. In 1917, a German politician claimed that...

Female freedom in England has destroyed all family life there. The women are so bad that more married men than single men offered themselves as recruits for the Army. The married men, in fact, join up to escape from their wives.

In one or two cases he may have been right!

French women were allowed to drink but only very weak wine.

If it sounds fun to be a British woman, then the working women paid a high price. They worked in dangerous war jobs where...

- 81 died in accidents
- 71 female workers died in explosions
- 61 died of poisoning

…and they were only paid half of a man's wages.

It's a fair cop

How did they get poisoned? By working with high explosives like TNT that got into their lungs and blood. The symptoms were...

- First your nose hurt, then it bled, your eyes stung and your throat became sore.

GOOD THING WE CAN OPENLY USE MAKE-UP NOW!

• You would get pains in the chest and stomach, diarrhoea and skin rashes.

• If you weren't treated, you'd get sickness, giddiness, swollen hands and feet, drowsiness and finally death.

But this didn't stop the women taking risks with the TNT. In September 1917, a young munitions worker was fined for stealing TNT from the factory where she worked. She stole it because it was common for workers to use TNT powder to give their hair a chestnut colour. But a red-head could become red-hot if you struck a match near her hair!

WAS SHE BLONDE? NO, BOMBED

Britain created its first policewomen during the First World War and one of their duties was to stop women workers taking explosives out of the factories, and to stop them taking cigarettes or matches *into* the factories. Policewoman Greta East kept a diary of her life on duty at a South Wales Munitions factory...

10 April 1917

The girls here are troublesome about bringing in cigarettes and matches. Last week a woman came to the Women Police Office and asked me to rescue her coat from the cloakroom as she had a train to catch. She said I'd recognize the coat because it had her payslip in the pocket. But, when I searched the pockets I found them full of cigarettes. Of course the poor wretch had to be prosecuted and fined. She must have forgotten about them.

A pretty dim worker, but not so dim as the underground toilets they had to use. Greta went on to describe the conditions…

> There are no drains because the ground is below sea level. The result is the toilets are a horrible and smelly swamp. There were no lights in the lavatories and those same lavatories are often full of rats and very dirty. The girls are afraid to go in.

With no lights how did you find the toilet paper? Or how did you avoid reaching out for toilet paper and picking up a rat by mistake? Yeuch!

By the end of the war, 30 police forces had appointed women – another First World War idea that is still with us. (Though some, like Manchester, refused.)

Warring women

Not all women were happy to 'serve' by making shells. In September 1914, French newspapers reported the story of a 28-year-old laundry woman who had been discovered fighting at the front in the uniform of a French soldier. She was sent back to her old job at the laundry but protested angrily. (Just like most people, she probably hated all the ironing.)

There is a story that a British woman also got as far as the trenches, dressed in the kilt of a Highland soldier. (This was very suitable because the Germans called the Highlanders 'ladies from Hell'.) She did it for a bet but was caught and returned to Britain.

By 1917 the Russian army was so weak it created a women's battalion, 'The Battalion of Death', to help. Three hundred women were led by the incredible Maria Botchkareva. Maria had been married at 15 and suffered terribly at the hands of two brutal husbands. War was wonderful compared to what she endured at home! She suffered frostbite and several wounds but survived. (She probably volunteered for the pleasure of being able to shoot at men!)

Battling babes

There are many stories of boys going into army recruiting offices to join up even though they were under age. Many army recruiting officers were willing to let them join anyway. Of course it was their duty to check on the age and reject the ones who *said* they were under age. This story is true and happened hundreds of times all over the world…

Parents were able to 'claim out' their sons if they could trace them, and the boy soldiers were sent home.

- Myer Rosenblum from London joined the London Welsh Regiment in August 1914, aged 13 years and nine months, but was 'claimed out' by his father in October 1914. He joined up again and was sent to Gallipoli, where he was wounded in June 1915. His father claimed him again when he was sent back to England.

- Private James Bartaby joined the 7th East Surreys, as a volunteer, on 20 January 1915, aged 13 years and ten months. After training, he went to France in late May and was wounded and sent home in October 1915.

- In October 1915, Arthur Peyman – 'described as 19 years of age' – was in court, charged with being absent from his regiment since the end of August. During the case, his mother appeared and produced his birth certificate, showing that he was only 14 years old.

At least Arthur Peyman escaped being shot for leaving his regiment. Other boys were not so lucky.

Trench tot

It wasn't just the fighting boys who ended up in the trenches. Sometimes small children were caught up in the battlefields. In early 1916, Philip Impey was going back into the trenches near La Basse, when he found a small girl abandoned in a ditch. He couldn't take her to safety and he couldn't leave her, so Philip picked her up and carried her into the trenches.

During the week, she climbed on to the parapet in full view of the Germans, who were close by. German soldiers shouted to her, offering her sweets and chocolate.

When the soldiers left the front, they took her with them. She was eventually sent to England and survived. Sadly, Philip Impey was killed in action soon after.

Cheeky Charlies

British kids in 1917 were getting out of control. There was a huge increase in vandalism, theft and street crimes among school-aged children.

- Some people blamed the fact that their fathers were away in the army.
- Others blamed the cinema. (Nowadays they'd blame social media, so nothing much changes, does it?)
- A third excuse was weak teachers – old ladies, brought out of retirement, to take the place of the men who had gone off to fight. (Imagine that! Kids taking advantage of their tough teacher being away. You wouldn't do a thing like that, would you?)

In Germany, the children had a surprise when the war started. In Berlin, all English teachers were sacked! (But that was wartime, so don't raise your hopes that it may happen for you!)

But by 1917 German children were so hungry they had a desperate new game ... stealing any food they could find.

Wrinklies at war

- The oldest French soldier was 78 years old.
- Italy's oldest soldier was 74.
- Lieutenant Henry Webber was, at 67, the oldest British soldier killed in action at the Somme in July 1916.
- In 1915, James White of Sowerby Bridge was sent home when it was found he had fought the Zulu War of 1878 and was 70 years old.

- In June 1918, the *Yorkshire Evening Press* told the story of a merchant sailor, William Jessop of Hull. He was 72 years old and had been torpedoed seven times.

William said…

Young men sometimes refuse to sail with me because they think I am unlucky.

OK JESSOP, THIS TIME FOR SURE

- In 1915, Chief Gunner Israel Harding had his left leg broken when his ship was blown up in the Dardanelles, near Turkey. He was 84 years old. He had once been a trawlerman but had run away to join the Royal Navy and first saw active service in the Crimean War of 1853–56.

Frightful flu facts

By November 1918, the war had killed about eight-and-a-half million people. But that was nothing compared to what happened next. Spanish flu spread around the world...

- People collapsed in the streets, at work and at home.
- It appeared to hit young, healthy people more than the old or very young.
- The deadly virus attacked the lungs, which hardened, making breathing impossible: the victim finally drowned in their own fluid.
- At the moment of death, virus-laden fluid poured out of the victim's mouth and nose.
- By May 1919, Spanish flu had killed over 200,000 in the UK and 20 million around the world – far more in one year than the war had managed in four.

- It killed more people than the Black Death.
- No one knew where it came from or why it suddenly went away.

Some men survived four years of shells, bullets and bombs only to get home safely … and die of the flu!

Strange but true

US soldier Major Harry S Truman kept his battalion guns firing 'til the last seconds of the First World War.

Nearly 30 years later, the Major was US President Harry S Truman. He ordered the dropping of atomic bombs on two Japanese cities. This brought the Second World War to an end.

In a strange way, you could say the same man fired the last shots in the two world wars.

TEST YOUR TEACHER...

Try this quick quiz on your teacher and watch as they strain their brain cell to the limit. If they get a question wrong, you can jeer because they're a dunce — if they get it right, you can jeer because they're probably old enough to remember the First World War!

1 If you lived in Britain in 1916 and wanted to know what it was like in the trenches, you could visit some. Where?

a) On the French side of the Western Front near the town of Ypres.

b) Behind the German lines, near Berlin.

c) In Blackpool.

2 A British minister in charge of food production was called what?
a) The Controller of Potatoes.
b) The Fat Controller.
c) Director of Army Food Transportation (DAFT).

3 Soldiers had an average of 20 lice crawling over their bodies. But what was the record?
a) 428.
b) 1,428.
c) 10,428.

I DON'T KNOW WHAT'S WORSE, HAVING THEM OR HAVING TO COUNT THEM

4 French newspapers of 1914 had reports that their soldiers were very comfortable in the trenches with what?

a) Wine.

b) Women.

c) Central heating.

5 What was a 'wibble-wobble'?

a) A soldier's name for a fat general.

b) Another name for a tank.

c) A horse with an injured leg.

6 The women who worked with TNT explosive were given the nickname 'canaries'. Why?

a) They were so happy they sang like canaries while they worked.

b) The TNT caused their hair to turn canary yellow.

c) Because the factory owners were getting 'cheep' labour.

7 The First World War changed fashions and almost killed off one fashion. What?

a) Men wearing top hats to work.

b) Women wearing knickers.

c) Children wearing wooden clogs.

8 Kaiser Wilhelm of Germany was a powerful but crazy king. What was his hobby?

a) Pulling the wings off flies.

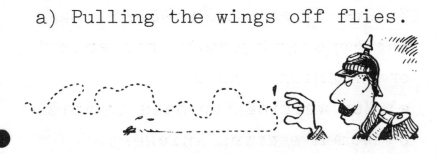

b) Throwing darts at pictures of his grandmother, Queen Victoria.

c) Chopping down trees.

9 Brit Patrick Gara was arrested for trying to dodge joining the army. His excuse was...

a) His mum wouldn't let him.

b) He was a coward and was afraid of getting hurt.

c) He didn't know there was a war on.

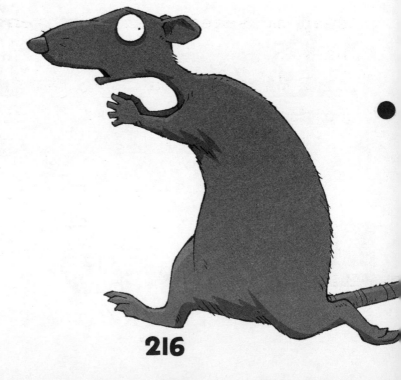

10 Brits with hard tennis courts were suspected by the police. Why?

a) Police believed they had been prepared as gun platforms for an invasion.

b) Tennis parties were a good cover for two spies to meet and swap messages hidden in tennis balls.

c) Police thought they were up to some secret racket.

Answers

1c) That's right, Blackpool. Soldiers recovering from wounds built replicas of the trenches at Loos. (That was a battlefield on the Western Front, not a toilet.) German people could visit the same sort of thing in Berlin.

2a) Imagine being called the Controller of Potatoes! Think of all the jokers who'd write to you and say, 'My potatoes are very naughty. Can you control them for me?'

MAN WITH LICE
(OR LICE WITH MAN)

3c) As well as having 10,428 lice in his shirt, there were about 10,253 lice eggs waiting to hatch. The same man would have had thousands more in his trousers, socks and hair. It's surprising he had any blood left after the lice had had their lunch!

4c) The truth is the soldiers in the trenches had to be very careful about lighting fires. The smoke gave enemy gunners something to aim at. So you could light a fire and be shelled to death, or not light a fire and freeze to death!

5b) The army name for a tank was a 'landship', but they collected lots of other names too: Slug, Whale, Toad, Tortoise, Land-crab, Behemoth, Boojum. Newspapers couldn't give away the secret by showing pictures, so Brit writers described a 'long, low, dust-coloured tortoise' while French newspapers reported they were equipped in front with 'some kind of cow catcher'. But to most soldiers it looked like a water 'tank' and that name stuck.

6b) TNT caused nasty skin rashes and its fumes turned the girls' hair bright mustard yellow – the colour of canaries. These unfortunate girls were often refused service in restaurants whose owners said, 'You are *unsightly*. Go away because you are putting the other customers off their food!'

7a) War changed British ways of life – posh people who would never have dreamed of travelling on a tram or bus before 1914, now travelled to work every day … paying their fares to 'conductorettes'. Women's fashion changed as a shortage of steel ended the wearing of tight corsets. City gents stopped wearing top hats as they were a nuisance on a bus or underground train with a low roof.

8c) Willy enjoyed felling trees at his palace at Potsdam. He was mad about stripping off the bark – which proves he was barking mad.

9b) In 1916, Patrick Gara was up before magistrates in Selby, Yorkshire, for avoiding military service. He was asked why he had not joined the army. He replied that he thought that he was safer in Selby than in the trenches! He was fined £2 and escorted to the nearest barracks. A year later, a man called

Graham Whitlaw was up before the magistrates in London for not reporting for military service. His excuse was that he was a duke and a bishop and he had been appointed Chief of the Army. He'd been appointed by King George IV (who had been dead almost 100 years). Of course Whitlaw was trying to act as if he was too mad to serve. It didn't work.

10a) Daft, but true. What use would a gun platform be in someone's back garden? You could always shell your neighbour's peas, I suppose.

BUT DARLING, EVERYONE'S GOT ONE!

Epilogue

There were lots of tragedies in the First World War. Almost every family in Britain, France, Germany and Russia lost someone. You can go to any town or village and see the names of the dead, carved on stone memorials. Many of the men who joined together died together and left their home towns desolate.

But that wasn't the *real* tragedy. The cruellest thing of all was that the First World War *didn't* solve any problems and it *didn't* bring peace. It led to the Second World War and far, far more misery, death and destruction.

Those whose names are carved on the memorials believed they were fighting for peace. Many would have given their lives gladly if they knew they had died in 'the war to end all wars'.

What went wrong? Big mistakes and small accidents. One accident so small that no one noticed it at the time. It happened in a German dugout during the Battle of the Somme. A British shell smashed into the trench and killed most of the Germans in it. But by a hideous chance, one German escaped with just a shell splinter in his face. He lived. He lived to start another war. His name was Adolf Hitler. Lucky Hitler – unlucky world.

Sometimes history is changed by great events like the First World War – sometimes it is changed by freak accidents in a fraction of a second: the arrow that hit King Harold at the Battle of Hastings and … the shell that *failed* to kill Hitler.

History can be horrible. But each of us should find our nearest war memorial, stand in front of it and read the names.

Then say, 'Never again.'

If everyone says that, and means it, then the deaths will not have been such a waste.

FRIGHTFUL FIRST WORLD WAR

Quiz

Beastly battles

There were lots of famous fights and crazy campaigns throughout the war. See if you can figure out which of these beastly battle facts are true and which are false.

1 The Battle of Mons began on 23 August 1914, one of the earliest big actions of the First World War. British soldiers later claimed they were protected during the battle by a group of angels. True or false?

2 French soldiers were taken to the front line for the Battle of the Marne in September 1914 by taxi. True or false?

3 There were three major battles around Ypres in Belgium throughout the war. In the last battle there, a young Winston Churchill – the great Second World War leader – was almost blinded in a gas attack. True or false?

4 The Battle of the Somme began on 1 July 1916 and went on until 18 November. The French and British attacked German lines. In that time the British suffered 57,470 casualties. True or false?

5 The French and British attack at Arras began on 1 October 1914. It was a failure for the Allies because they only managed to capture a single hill. True or false?

Terrible trenches quick quiz

Take this quick quiz to find out if you would have survived life in the terrible trenches or been beaten and left in bits.

1 Poisonous gas was used for the first time in the First World War. What would you do if you were caught in a gas attack in the trenches? (Clue: you might need a wee bit of help)

2 How could you tell when an enemy bombardment was about to begin? (Clue: vile vermin)

3 Trench toilets were buckets or holes dug into the mud. With hundreds of soldiers suffering from deadly dysentery, they filled up quickly. Where could you go to poo if the foul latrines were full? (Clue: a number two in no-man's land?)

4 Things could get pretty chilly in the trenches and lots of icy infantry soldiers suffered from frostbite. How did they save their frozen feet? (Clue: you'll get snow help from me!)

5 Trench foot was caused by cold, damp and unhealthy conditions (the trenches were filled with mud and water and poo and bodies). What could you do to prevent having your feet chopped off because of this disgusting disease? (Clue: grease is the word)

Answers

Beastly battles

1 True. The British managed to beat back the Germans despite being outnumbered and they thought that God had sent a ghostly army of angels to help them. To this day no one really knows the truth about the Angels of Mons...

2 True. France ordered every taxi cab in Paris to be available to take soldiers to the frontline so they would get there in time for the big battle.

3 False. It was a young Adolf Hitler who was smothered by the ghastly gas. In the whole of the First World War horrid Hitler was awarded six medals for bravery!

4 False. The casualty figure of nearly 58,000 was for the first day alone – 1 July. This is still a record.

5 False. It was a success for the Allies because they managed to capture a single hill. That hill, known as Vimy Ridge, captured by Canadian forces, was very important!

Terrible trenches quick quiz

1 Pee on your hanky and then tie it over your nose and mouth. This weird wee trick really worked – the chemicals in urine kept out the gas.

2 Watch the rats. Rats were everywhere in the stinking trenches and soldiers believed that they knew instinctively when an attack was about to happen and disappeared. If you couldn't see a rotten rat then you were probably in for a beastly bombardment.

3 A shell-hole. Who needed specially dug holes when the Germans made them for you with their bombs? Just find a cosy shell hole and squat.

4 Rubbing them with snow. In fact we now know that rubbing frostbite with anything actually makes the damage worse. So rubbing it with snow was not only parky and painful it was also pointless!

5 Cover your feet with grease made from whale oil. A single battalion in the trenches could use up to ten gallons of gooey grease every day!

Interesting Index

237